Frappe Recipe Book

By CARLA HUTSON

Table of Contents

Roasted Red Pepper Tomato Basil Frappe

Savor the savory goodness of this Roasted Red Pepper Tomato Basil Frappe. Packed with antioxidants and flavors, this unique frappe is a refreshing twist on a classic combination.

TOTAL TIME COOKING: 12 minutes

Ingredients:

- 1/2 cup roasted red peppers
- 1 cup cherry tomatoes
- Handful of fresh basil leaves
- 1 cup vegetable broth (cooled)
- Juice of 1 lemon
- 1 tablespoon agave syrup or honey
- 1 cup ice cubes

Directions:

1. combine roasted red peppers, cherry tomatoes, basil leaves, vegetable broth, lemon juice, agave syrup, and ice cubes in a blender.
2. Blend until smooth and savory.
3. Pour into a glass and enjoy the unique and refreshing frappe.

Coconut Acai Berry Protein Frappe

Elevate your protein intake with this Coconut Acai Berry Protein Frappe. Packed with the superfood benefits of acai berries and the richness of coconut, this frappe is a delicious and nutritious choice.

TOTAL TIME COOKING: 10 minutes

Ingredients:

- 1/2 cup acai berries (frozen or puree)
- 1 scoop of plant-based protein powder
- 1 cup coconut water
- 1 tablespoon chia seeds
- 1 tablespoon agave syrup or any sweetener of choice
- 1 cup ice cubes

Directions:

1. combine acai berries, protein powder, coconut water, chia seeds, agave syrup, and ice cubes in a blender.
2. Blend until smooth and protein-packed.
3. Pour into a glass and enjoy the tropical and nutritious frappe.

Spinach Pineapple Ginger Detox Frappe

Cleanse and refresh with this Spinach Pineapple Ginger Detox Frappe. Packed with detoxifying ingredients, this frappe is a zesty and health-conscious beverage.

TOTAL TIME COOKING: 8 minutes

Ingredients:

- Handful of fresh spinach leaves
- 1 cup pineapple chunks
- 1 teaspoon fresh ginger, grated
- Juice of 1 lime
- 1 cup coconut water
- 1 tablespoon agave syrup or honey
- 1 cup ice cubes

Directions:

1. combine spinach leaves, pineapple chunks, fresh ginger, lime juice, coconut water, agave syrup, and ice cubes in a blender.
2. Blend until smooth and revitalizing.
3. Pour into a glass and enjoy the zesty and detoxifying frappe.

Broccoli Blueberry Mint Frappe

Experience a unique combination of nutrients with this Broccoli Blueberry Mint Frappe. Packed with antioxidants and the freshness of mint, this frappe is a wholesome and vibrant choice.

TOTAL TIME COOKING: 10 minutes

Ingredients:

- 1/2 cup cooked broccoli florets
- 1/2 cup blueberries (fresh or frozen)
- Handful of fresh mint leaves
- 1 cup almond milk
- 1 tablespoon agave syrup or any sweetener of choice
- 1 cup ice cubes

Directions:

1. combine cooked broccoli florets, blueberries, fresh mint leaves, almond milk, agave syrup, and ice cubes in a blender.
2. Blend until smooth and nutrient-dense.
3. Pour into a glass and enjoy the unique and wholesome frappe.

Lemon Turmeric Coconut Water Frappe

Invigorate your senses with this lemon, turmeric, and coconut water frappe. Packed with the anti-inflammatory benefits of turmeric and the hydrating properties of coconut water, this frappe is a refreshing and health-conscious choice.

TOTAL TIME COOKING: 8 minutes

Ingredients:

- Juice of 2 lemons
- 1/2 teaspoon ground turmeric
- 1 cup coconut water
- 1 tablespoon agave syrup or honey
- 1 cup ice cubes

Directions:

1. combine lemon juice, ground turmeric, coconut water, agave syrup, and ice cubes in a blender.
2. Blend until smooth and refreshing.
3. Pour into a glass and enjoy the zesty and healthful frappe.

Classic Coffee Frappe

Indulge in the rich and refreshing taste of this classic coffee frappe. Perfect for a quick pick-me-up on a warm day.

TOTAL TIME COOKING: 10 minutes

Ingredients:

- 1 cup brewed coffee, cooled
- 1 cup milk
- 2 tablespoons sugar
- 1 cup ice cubes
- Whipped cream (optional)
- Chocolate syrup (optional)

Directions:

1. combine brewed coffee, milk, sugar, and ice cubes in a blender.
2. Blend until smooth and creamy.
3. Pour into a glass and top with whipped cream and chocolate syrup if desired.

Chocolate Banana Frappe

Satisfy your sweet cravings with this refreshing frappe's delightful combination of chocolate and banana.

TOTAL TIME COOKING: 15 minutes

Ingredients:

- 1 ripe banana
- 2 tablespoons cocoa powder
- 1 cup milk
- 2 tablespoons sugar
- 1 cup ice cubes
- Chocolate shavings (optional)

Directions:

1. combine banana, cocoa powder, milk, sugar, and ice cubes in a blender.
2. Blend until smooth and creamy.
3. Garnish with chocolate shavings if desired.

Mint Chocolate Chip Frappe

Experience a burst of freshness with the cool, minty flavor and chocolatey goodness of this delightful frappe.

TOTAL TIME COOKING: 12 minutes

Ingredients:

- 1 cup brewed coffee, cooled
- 1 cup milk
- 1/2 teaspoon mint extract
- 2 tablespoons chocolate chips
- 2 tablespoons sugar
- 1 cup ice cubes
- Whipped cream (optional)

Directions:

1. combine brewed coffee, milk, mint extract, chocolate chips, sugar, and ice cubes in a blender.
2. Blend until smooth and creamy.
3. Top with whipped cream if desired.

Vanilla Almond Frappe

Indulge in the velvety smoothness of vanilla and the nutty richness of almonds with this luscious frappe.

TOTAL TIME COOKING: 8 minutes

Ingredients:

- 1 cup brewed coffee, cooled
- 1 cup milk
- 1 teaspoon vanilla extract
- 2 tablespoons almond butter
- 2 tablespoons sugar
- 1 cup ice cubes
- Sliced almonds (for garnish)

Directions:

1. combine brewed coffee, milk, vanilla extract, almond butter, sugar, and ice cubes in a blender.
2. Blend until smooth and creamy.
3. Garnish with sliced almonds.

Berry Blast Frappe

Enjoy the vibrant flavors of mixed berries in this energizing and antioxidant-packed frappe.

TOTAL TIME COOKING: 10 minutes

Ingredients:

- 1/2 cup mixed berries (strawberries, blueberries, raspberries)
- 1 cup milk
- 2 tablespoons honey
- 1 cup ice cubes
- Fresh berries (for garnish)

Directions:

1. combine mixed berries, milk, honey, and ice cubes in a blender.
2. Blend until smooth and vibrant.
3. Garnish with fresh berries.

Caramel Macchiato Frappe

Indulge in the perfect balance of rich coffee, creamy milk, and luscious caramel with this irresistible frappe.

TOTAL TIME COOKING: 15 minutes

Ingredients:

- 1 cup brewed espresso, cooled
- 1 cup milk
- 2 tablespoons caramel sauce
- 2 tablespoons sugar
- 1 cup ice cubes
- Whipped cream (optional)
- Caramel drizzle (optional)

Directions:

1. combine brewed espresso, milk, caramel sauce, sugar, and ice cubes in a blender.
2. Blend until smooth and creamy.
3. Top with whipped cream and a drizzle of caramel if desired.

Coconut Mocha Frappe

Escape to a tropical paradise with the exotic coconut and rich mocha blend in this refreshing frappe.

TOTAL TIME COOKING: 12 minutes

Ingredients:

- 1 cup brewed coffee, cooled
- 1 cup coconut milk
- 2 tablespoons chocolate syrup
- 2 tablespoons sugar
- 1 cup ice cubes
- Shredded coconut (for garnish)

Directions:

1. combine brewed coffee, coconut milk, chocolate syrup, sugar, and ice cubes in a blender.
2. Blend until smooth and creamy.
3. Garnish with shredded coconut.

Pumpkin Spice Frappe

Embrace the cozy fall flavors with the warm and aromatic notes of pumpkin spice in this delightful frappe.

TOTAL TIME COOKING: 10 minutes

Ingredients:

- 1 cup brewed coffee, cooled
- 1/2 cup pumpkin puree
- 1 cup milk
- 2 tablespoons maple syrup
- 1 teaspoon pumpkin spice
- 1 cup ice cubes
- Whipped cream and cinnamon (for garnish)

Directions:

1. combine brewed coffee, pumpkin puree, milk, maple syrup, pumpkin spice, and ice cubes in a blender.
2. Blend until smooth and creamy.
3. Top with whipped cream and a sprinkle of cinnamon.

Hazelnut Chocolate Frappe

Indulge in the nutty goodness of hazelnut combined with the rich flavor of chocolate in this decadent frappe.

TOTAL TIME COOKING: 15 minutes

Ingredients:

- 1 cup brewed coffee, cooled
- 1 cup milk
- 2 tablespoons chocolate hazelnut spread
- 2 tablespoons sugar
- 1 cup ice cubes
- Chopped hazelnuts (for garnish)

Directions:

1. combine brewed coffee, milk, chocolate hazelnut spread, sugar, and ice cubes in a blender.
2. Blend until smooth and creamy.
3. Garnish with chopped hazelnuts.

Matcha Green Tea Frappe

Experience a burst of antioxidants and a hint of earthy sweetness with this vibrant matcha green tea frappe.

TOTAL TIME COOKING: 8 minutes

Ingredients:

- 1 cup milk
- 1 tablespoon matcha green tea powder
- 2 tablespoons honey
- 1 cup ice cubes
- Matcha powder (for garnish)

Directions:

1. combine milk, matcha green tea powder, honey, and ice cubes in a blender.
2. Blend until smooth and vibrant.
3. Sprinkle matcha powder on top for garnish.

Raspberry White Chocolate Frappe

Experience the perfect blend of tart raspberries and sweet white chocolate in this heavenly frappe.

TOTAL TIME COOKING: 12 minutes

Ingredients:

- 1/2 cup fresh or frozen raspberries
- 1 cup milk
- 2 tablespoons white chocolate chips
- 2 tablespoons sugar
- 1 cup ice cubes
- White chocolate shavings (for garnish)

Directions:

1. combine raspberries, milk, white chocolate chips, sugar, and ice cubes in a blender.
2. Blend until smooth and creamy.
3. Garnish with white chocolate shavings.

Iced Chai Tea Frappe

Savor the aromatic spices of chai tea in a cool and refreshing frappe for a delightful twist on a classic beverage.

TOTAL TIME COOKING: 10 minutes

Ingredients:

- 1 cup brewed chai tea, cooled
- 1 cup milk
- 2 tablespoons honey
- 1 cup ice cubes
- Ground cinnamon (for garnish)

Directions:

1. combine brewed chai tea, milk, honey, and ice cubes in a blender.
2. Blend until smooth and frothy.
3. Sprinkle ground cinnamon on top for garnish.

Tropical Pineapple Coconut Frappe

Transport yourself to a tropical paradise with the exotic flavors of pineapple and coconut in this refreshing frappe.

TOTAL TIME COOKING: 15 minutes

Ingredients:

- 1 cup pineapple chunks (fresh or frozen)
- 1 cup coconut milk
- 2 tablespoons coconut flakes
- 2 tablespoons honey
- 1 cup ice cubes
- Pineapple wedge (for garnish)

Directions:

1. combine pineapple chunks, coconut milk, coconut flakes, honey, and ice cubes in a blender.
2. Blend until smooth and tropical.
3. Garnish with a pineapple wedge.

Mocha Hazelnut Frappe

Indulge in the perfect marriage of chocolate and hazelnut with this rich and velvety mocha hazelnut frappe.

TOTAL TIME COOKING: 12 minutes

Ingredients:

- 1 cup brewed coffee, cooled
- 1 cup milk
- 2 tablespoons chocolate syrup
- 2 tablespoons hazelnut syrup
- 1 cup ice cubes
- Whipped cream and crushed hazelnuts (for garnish)

Directions:

1. combine brewed coffee, milk, chocolate syrup, hazelnut syrup, and ice cubes in a blender.
2. Blend until smooth and indulgent.
3. Top with whipped cream and crushed hazelnuts.

Blueberry Lemonade Frappe

Refresh your taste buds with the vibrant combination of sweet blueberries and zesty lemonade in this invigorating frappe.

TOTAL TIME COOKING: 10 minutes

Ingredients:

- 1/2 cup fresh or frozen blueberries
- 1 cup lemonade
- 2 tablespoons sugar
- 1 cup ice cubes
- Lemon slices (for garnish)

Directions:

1. combine blueberries, lemonade, sugar, and ice cubes in a blender.
2. Blend until smooth and refreshing.
3. Garnish with lemon slices.

Salted Caramel Pretzel Frappe

Indulge in this delightful frappe's perfect balance of sweet and salty with the decadent combination of salted caramel and crunchy pretzels.

TOTAL TIME COOKING: 15 minutes

Ingredients:

- 1 cup brewed coffee, cooled
- 1 cup milk
- 2 tablespoons salted caramel sauce
- 2 tablespoons crushed pretzels
- 2 tablespoons sugar
- 1 cup ice cubes
- Whipped cream and additional pretzels (for garnish)

Directions:

1. combine brewed coffee, milk, salted caramel sauce, crushed pretzels, sugar, and ice cubes in a blender.
2. Blend until smooth and heavenly.
3. Top with whipped cream and garnish with pretzels.

Cookies and Cream Frappe

Experience the classic combination of chocolate cookies and creamy goodness in this indulgent, satisfying frappe.

TOTAL TIME COOKING: 12 minutes

Ingredients:

- 1 cup brewed coffee, cooled
- 1 cup milk
- 3 chocolate sandwich cookies
- 2 tablespoons chocolate syrup
- 1 cup ice cubes
- Crushed cookies (for garnish)

Directions:

1. combine brewed coffee, milk, chocolate sandwich cookies, chocolate syrup, and ice cubes in a blender.
2. Blend until smooth and creamy.
3. Garnish with crushed cookies.

Spiced Apple Pie Frappe

Capture the essence of a comforting apple pie with the warm spices and fruity goodness in this delightful spiced apple pie frappe.

TOTAL TIME COOKING: 15 minutes

Ingredients:

- 1 cup apple juice
- 1/2 cup applesauce
- 1 cup milk
- 2 tablespoons maple syrup
- 1/2 teaspoon cinnamon
- 1 cup ice cubes
- Whipped cream and a sprinkle of cinnamon (for garnish)

Directions:

1. combine apple juice, applesauce, milk, maple syrup, cinnamon, and ice cubes in a blender.
2. Blend until smooth and comforting.
3. Top with whipped cream and sprinkle cinnamon on top.

Pistachio Rose Frappe

Elevate your frappe experience with the unique combination of pistachio and delicate rose flavors for a refreshing and sophisticated twist.

TOTAL TIME COOKING: 10 minutes

Ingredients:

- 1 cup milk
- 2 tablespoons pistachio paste or ground pistachios
- 1 tablespoon rose water
- 2 tablespoons honey
- 1 cup ice cubes
- Chopped pistachios (for garnish)

Directions:

1. combine milk, pistachio paste, rose water, honey, and ice cubes in a blender.
2. Blend until smooth and aromatic.
3. Garnish with chopped pistachios.

Cherry Vanilla Frappe

Enjoy the sweet and fruity flavor of cherries paired with the classic elegance of vanilla in this delightful and visually appealing frappe.

TOTAL TIME COOKING: 12 minutes

Ingredients:

- 1/2 cup fresh or frozen cherries, pitted
- 1 cup milk
- 1 teaspoon vanilla extract
- 2 tablespoons sugar
- 1 cup ice cubes
- Maraschino cherry (for garnish)

Directions:

1. combine cherries, milk, vanilla extract, sugar, and ice cubes in a blender.
2. Blend until smooth and vibrant.
3. Garnish with a maraschino cherry.

Maple Pecan Pie Frappe

Savor the cozy flavors of fall with this indulgent Maple Pecan Pie Frappe, blending the richness of pecans and the sweetness of maple syrup.

TOTAL TIME COOKING: 15 minutes

Ingredients:

- 1 cup brewed coffee, cooled
- 1 cup milk
- 2 tablespoons maple syrup
- 2 tablespoons chopped pecans
- 1 tablespoon caramel sauce
- 1 cup ice cubes
- Whipped cream and additional pecans (for garnish)

Directions:

1. combine brewed coffee, milk, maple syrup, chopped pecans, caramel sauce, and ice cubes in a blender.
2. Blend until smooth and comforting.
3. Top with whipped cream and garnish with additional pecans.

Orange Creamsicle Frappe

Experience an orange creamsicle's nostalgic and refreshing taste in this delightful frappe, perfect for a sunny day.

TOTAL TIME COOKING: 10 minutes

Ingredients:

- 1 cup orange juice
- 1 cup vanilla ice cream
- 1/2 cup milk
- 2 tablespoons honey
- 1 cup ice cubes
- Orange zest (for garnish)

Directions:

1. combine orange juice, vanilla ice cream, milk, honey, and ice cubes in a blender.
2. Blend until smooth and creamy.
3. Garnish with orange zest.

Cinnamon Toast Crunch Frappe

Indulge your taste buds with the nostalgic flavor of cinnamon toast crunch cereal in this creative and satisfying frappe.

TOTAL TIME COOKING: 12 minutes

Ingredients:

- 1 cup brewed coffee, cooled
- 1 cup milk
- 2 tablespoons cinnamon sugar
- 1/2 cup cinnamon toast crunch cereal
- 1 cup ice cubes
- Whipped cream and a sprinkle of cinnamon (for garnish)

Directions:

1. combine brewed coffee, milk, cinnamon sugar, cinnamon toast, crunch cereal, and ice cubes in a blender.
2. Blend until smooth and reminiscent of childhood.
3. Top with whipped cream and a sprinkle of cinnamon.

Pineapple Mint Mojito Frappe

Escape to a tropical paradise with this refreshing Pineapple Mint Mojito Frappe, blending the sweetness of pineapple with the coolness of mint.

TOTAL TIME COOKING: 15 minutes

Ingredients:

- 1 cup pineapple chunks (fresh or frozen)
- 1 cup coconut water
- 1 tablespoon fresh mint leaves
- 2 tablespoons honey
- 1 cup ice cubes
- Mint sprig (for garnish)

Directions:

1. combine pineapple chunks, coconut water, fresh mint leaves, honey, and ice cubes in a blender.
2. Blend until smooth and revitalizing.
3. Garnish with a mint sprig.

Black Forest Frappe

Indulge in the decadent combination of chocolate and cherries with this Black Forest Frappe, reminiscent of the classic cake.

TOTAL TIME COOKING: 12 minutes

Ingredients:

- 1 cup brewed coffee, cooled
- 1 cup milk
- 2 tablespoons chocolate syrup
- 1/4 cup pitted cherries (fresh or frozen)
- 1 cup ice cubes
- Whipped cream and chocolate shavings (for garnish)

Directions:

1. combine brewed coffee, milk, chocolate syrup, pitted cherries, and ice cubes in a blender.
2. Blend until smooth and luxurious.
3. Top with whipped cream and chocolate shavings.

Tiramisu Frappe

Indulge in the classic Italian dessert flavors with this Tiramisu Frappe, combining the richness of coffee and the creaminess of mascarpone.

TOTAL TIME COOKING: 15 minutes

Ingredients:

- 1 cup brewed espresso, cooled
- 1 cup milk
- 2 tablespoons mascarpone cheese
- 2 tablespoons chocolate syrup
- 1 tablespoon instant coffee powder
- 1 cup ice cubes
- Cocoa powder (for garnish)

Directions:

1. combine brewed espresso, milk, mascarpone cheese, chocolate syrup, instant coffee powder, and ice cubes in a blender.
2. Blend until smooth and velvety.
3. Dust with cocoa powder for garnish.

Lavender Honey Almond Frappe

Experience a unique floral twist with this Lavender Honey Almond Frappe, blending the delicate notes of lavender with the richness of almonds.

TOTAL TIME COOKING: 12 minutes

Ingredients:

- 1 cup almond milk
- 1/2 teaspoon dried lavender buds (culinary grade)
- 2 tablespoons honey
- 1/4 cup almond butter
- 1 cup ice cubes
- Lavender sprig (for garnish)

Directions:

1. warm almond milk with dried lavender buds in a small saucepan. Allow it to steep for 5 minutes, then strain.
2. combine the lavender-infused almond milk, honey, almond butter, and ice cubes in a blender.
3. Blend until smooth and aromatic. Garnish with a lavender sprig.

Matcha Coconut Frappe

Enjoy the health benefits of matcha combined with the tropical twist of coconut in this refreshing Matcha Coconut Frappe.

TOTAL TIME COOKING: 10 minutes

Ingredients:

- 1 cup coconut milk
- 1 tablespoon matcha green tea powder
- 2 tablespoons agave syrup or honey
- 1 cup ice cubes
- Coconut flakes (for garnish)

Directions:

1. combine coconut milk, matcha green tea powder, agave syrup, and ice cubes in a blender.
2. Blend until smooth and vibrant.
3. Garnish with coconut flakes.

Honeydew Mint Frappe

Stay cool and refreshed with this Honeydew Mint Frappe, featuring the subtle sweetness of honeydew and the refreshing essence of mint.

TOTAL TIME COOKING: 12 minutes

Ingredients:

- 1 cup honeydew melon, diced
- 1 cup coconut water
- 2 tablespoons fresh mint leaves
- 1 tablespoon honey
- 1 cup ice cubes
- Mint leaves (for garnish)

Directions:

1. combine honeydew melon, coconut water, fresh mint leaves, honey, and ice cubes in a blender.
2. Blend until smooth and revitalizing.
3. Garnish with mint leaves.

Peanut Butter Banana Chocolate Frappe

Satisfy your sweet tooth with this indulgent Peanut Butter Banana Chocolate Frappe, combining the classic peanut butter and chocolate with the sweetness of banana.

TOTAL TIME COOKING: 15 minutes

Ingredients:

- 1 cup milk
- 1 ripe banana
- 2 tablespoons peanut butter
- 2 tablespoons chocolate syrup
- 1 cup ice cubes
- Crushed peanuts (for garnish)

Directions:

1. combine milk, ripe banana, peanut butter, chocolate syrup, and ice cubes in a blender.
2. Blend until smooth and creamy.
3. Garnish with crushed peanuts.

Vegan Vanilla Almond Frappe

Indulge in the creamy goodness of this Vegan Vanilla Almond Frappe. Combining vanilla and almond creates a luscious and satisfying drink without any dairy.

TOTAL TIME COOKING: 10 minutes

Ingredients:

- 1 cup almond milk
- 1 teaspoon vanilla extract
- 2 tablespoons almond butter
- 2 tablespoons agave syrup or any sweetener of choice
- 1 cup ice cubes
- Sliced almonds (for garnish)

Directions:

1. combine almond milk, vanilla extract, almond butter, agave syrup, and ice cubes in a blender.
2. Blend until smooth and velvety.
3. Garnish with sliced almonds.

Vegan Mocha Banana Frappe

Enjoy the rich and chocolatey goodness of this Vegan Mocha Banana Frappe. Combining coffee, banana, and cocoa creates a delightful treat for your taste buds.

TOTAL TIME COOKING: 12 minutes

Ingredients:

- 1 cup brewed coffee, cooled
- 1 ripe banana
- 2 tablespoons cocoa powder
- 1 cup almond milk
- 2 tablespoons agave syrup or any sweetener of choice
- 1 cup ice cubes
- Cacao nibs (for garnish)

Directions:

1. combine brewed coffee, ripe banana, cocoa powder, almond milk, agave syrup, and ice cubes in a blender.
2. Blend until smooth and indulgent.
3. Garnish with cacao nibs.

Vegan Berry Coconut Frappe

Embrace the tropical and fruity vibes with this Vegan Berry Coconut Frappe. Packed with antioxidants, it's a refreshing and guilt-free delight.

TOTAL TIME COOKING: 10 minutes

Ingredients:

- 1/2 cup mixed berries (strawberries, blueberries, raspberries)
- 1 cup coconut milk
- 2 tablespoons agave syrup or any sweetener of choice
- 1 cup ice cubes
- Shredded coconut (for garnish)

Directions:

1. combine mixed berries, coconut milk, agave syrup, and ice cubes in a blender.
2. Blend until smooth and vibrant.
3. Garnish with shredded coconut.

Vegan Matcha Mint Frappe

Elevate your frappe experience with this Vegan Matcha Mint Frappe. Mixing matcha green tea and refreshing mint creates a unique and energizing drink.

TOTAL TIME COOKING: 12 minutes

Ingredients:

- 1 cup almond milk
- 1 teaspoon matcha green tea powder
- 2 tablespoons fresh mint leaves
- 2 tablespoons agave syrup or any sweetener of choice
- 1 cup ice cubes
- Mint leaves (for garnish)

Directions:

1. combine almond milk, matcha green tea powder, fresh mint leaves, agave syrup, and ice cubes in a blender.
2. Blend until smooth and refreshing.
3. Garnish with mint leaves.

Vegan Chocolate Peanut Butter Frappe

Indulge your chocolate cravings with this Vegan Chocolate Peanut Butter Frappe. The combination of rich cocoa and creamy peanut butter creates a decadent treat.

TOTAL TIME COOKING: 15 minutes

Ingredients:

- 1 cup almond milk
- 2 tablespoons peanut butter
- 2 tablespoons cocoa powder
- 2 tablespoons agave syrup or any sweetener of choice
- 1 cup ice cubes
- Crushed peanuts (for garnish)

Directions:

1. combine almond milk, peanut butter, cocoa powder, agave syrup, and ice cubes in a blender.
2. Blend until smooth and indulgent.
3. Garnish with crushed peanuts.

Avocado Spinach Green Tea Frappe

Elevate your frappe experience with this Avocado Spinach Green Tea Frappe. Packed with antioxidants and healthy fats, this refreshing drink is nutritious for your taste buds.

TOTAL TIME COOKING: 10 minutes

Ingredients:

- 1 ripe avocado
- Handful of fresh spinach leaves
- 1 teaspoon matcha green tea powder
- 1 cup coconut water
- 1 tablespoon honey or agave syrup
- 1 cup ice cubes

Directions:

1. combine ripe avocado, fresh spinach leaves, matcha green tea powder, coconut water, honey, and ice cubes in a blender.
2. Blend until smooth and vibrant.
3. Pour into a glass and enjoy the green goodness.

Turmeric Ginger Mango Frappe

Boost your immune system with this Turmeric Ginger Mango Frappe. The turmeric's anti-inflammatory properties, combined with mango's tropical sweetness, create a flavorful and health-conscious beverage.

TOTAL TIME COOKING: 12 minutes

Ingredients:

- 1 cup mango chunks (fresh or frozen)
- 1 teaspoon turmeric powder
- 1 tablespoon fresh ginger, peeled and grated
- 1 cup almond milk
- 1 tablespoon maple syrup or agave syrup
- 1 cup ice cubes

Directions:

1. combine mango chunks, turmeric powder, fresh ginger, almond milk, maple syrup, and ice cubes in a blender.
2. Blend until smooth and refreshing.
3. Pour into a glass and savor the immune-boosting flavors.

Quinoa Banana Chia Frappe

Fuel your day with this Quinoa Banana Chia Frappe. Packed with protein and omega-3s, this nutritious frappe is a satisfying and energizing breakfast or snack option.

TOTAL TIME COOKING: 15 minutes (including quinoa preparation)

Ingredients:

- 1/2 cup cooked quinoa, cooled
- 1 ripe banana
- 2 tablespoons chia seeds
- 1 cup almond milk
- 1 tablespoon maple syrup or agave syrup
- 1 cup ice cubes

Directions:

1. combine cooked quinoa, ripe banana, chia seeds, almond milk, maple syrup, and ice cubes in a blender.
2. Blend until smooth and protein-packed.
3. Pour into a glass and enjoy this unique and nutritious frappe.

Blueberry Kale Almond Frappe

Experience a burst of antioxidants with this Blueberry Kale Almond Frappe. The combination of vibrant blueberries, nutrient-rich kale, and almonds make it a delicious and health-conscious choice.

TOTAL TIME COOKING: 10 minutes

Ingredients:

- 1/2 cup blueberries (fresh or frozen)
- Handful of kale leaves, stems removed
- 1/4 cup almonds
- 1 cup almond milk
- 1 tablespoon agave syrup or honey
- 1 cup ice cubes

Directions:

1. combine blueberries, kale leaves, almonds, almond milk, agave syrup, and ice cubes in a blender.
2. Blend until smooth and full of antioxidants.
3. Pour into a glass and relish the wholesome flavors.

Cucumber Mint Lime Frappe

Stay refreshed with this Cucumber Mint Lime Frappe. Hydrating cucumber, refreshing mint, and zesty lime create a light and revitalizing drink that is perfect for a hot day.

TOTAL TIME COOKING: 8 minutes

Ingredients:

- 1/2 cucumber, peeled and sliced
- Handful of fresh mint leaves
- Juice of 1 lime
- 1 cup coconut water
- 1 tablespoon agave syrup or honey
- 1 cup ice cubes

Directions:

1. combine cucumber slices, mint leaves, lime juice, coconut water, agave syrup, and ice cubes in a blender.
2. Blend until smooth and hydrating.
3. Pour into a glass and enjoy the cool and refreshing taste.

Pomegranate Basil Lemonade Frappe

Elevate your summer refreshment with this Pomegranate Basil Lemonade Frappe. Bursting with antioxidants and the aromatic essence of basil, this frappe is a delightful and healthy choice.

TOTAL TIME COOKING: 10 minutes

Ingredients:

- 1/2 cup pomegranate seeds
- Handful of fresh basil leaves
- Juice of 2 lemons
- 1 cup coconut water
- 1 tablespoon agave syrup or honey
- 1 cup ice cubes

Directions:

1. combine pomegranate seeds, fresh basil leaves, lemon juice, coconut water, agave syrup, and ice cubes in a blender.
2. Blend until smooth and refreshing.
3. Pour into a glass and enjoy the unique flavor combination.

Sweet Potato Spice Frappe

Experience the heartiness of this Sweet Potato Spice Frappe, combining the goodness of sweet potatoes with warming spices for a nutrient-rich and satisfying beverage.

TOTAL TIME COOKING: 15 minutes (including sweet potato preparation)

Ingredients:

- 1/2 cup cooked and cooled sweet potato
- 1 teaspoon ground cinnamon
- 1/4 teaspoon ground nutmeg
- 1 cup almond milk
- 1 tablespoon maple syrup or agave syrup
- 1 cup ice cubes

Directions:

1. combine cooked sweet potato, cinnamon, nutmeg, almond milk, maple syrup, and ice cubes in a blender.
2. Blend until smooth and hearty.
3. Pour into a glass and savor the unique flavors.

Mango Basil Coconut Water Frappe

Quench your thirst with this Mango Basil Coconut Water Frappe. The tropical sweetness of mango, paired with the herbal essence of basil and hydrating coconut water, makes for a revitalizing and healthy beverage.

TOTAL TIME COOKING: 8 minutes

Ingredients:

- 1 cup mango chunks (fresh or frozen)
- Handful of fresh basil leaves
- 1 cup coconut water
- 1 tablespoon agave syrup or honey
- 1 cup ice cubes

Directions:

1. combine mango chunks, fresh basil leaves, coconut water, agave syrup, and ice cubes in a blender.
2. Blend until smooth and hydrating.
3. Pour into a glass and enjoy the tropical goodness.

Almond Blue Spirulina Frappe

Boost your energy with this Almond Blue Spirulina Frappe. Packed with protein from almonds and the nutritional benefits of blue spirulina, this vibrant frappe is a nutrient powerhouse.

TOTAL TIME COOKING: 12 minutes

Ingredients:

- 1 cup almond milk
- 1/4 cup almonds
- 1 teaspoon blue spirulina powder
- 2 tablespoons agave syrup or any sweetener of choice
- 1 cup ice cubes

Directions:

1. combine almond milk, almonds, blue spirulina powder, agave syrup, and ice cubes in a blender.
2. Blend until smooth and protein-rich.
3. Pour into a glass and enjoy the vibrant color and nutrients.

Raspberry Oatmeal Protein Frappe

Start your day right with this Raspberry Oatmeal Protein Frappe. Packed with fiber from oats, the goodness of raspberries, and plant-based protein, this frappe is a nutritious and satisfying breakfast option.

TOTAL TIME COOKING: 15 minutes (including oatmeal preparation)

Ingredients:

- 1/2 cup rolled oats, cooked and cooled
- 1/2 cup fresh or frozen raspberries
- 1 cup almond milk
- 1 tablespoon chia seeds
- 1 tablespoon agave syrup or any sweetener of choice
- 1 cup ice cubes

Directions:

1. combine cooked oats, raspberries, almond milk, chia seeds, agave syrup, and ice cubes in a blender.
2. Blend until smooth and fiber-rich.
3. Pour into a glass and relish the nutritious start to your day.

Carrot Ginger Turmeric Frappe

Boost your immunity with this Carrot Ginger Turmeric Frappe. Packed with anti-inflammatory ingredients, carrots, ginger, and turmeric combine to create a flavorful and health-conscious beverage.

TOTAL TIME COOKING: 12 minutes

Ingredients:

- 1/2 cup chopped carrots
- 1 teaspoon fresh ginger, grated
- 1/2 teaspoon ground turmeric
- 1 cup coconut water
- 1 tablespoon agave syrup or honey
- 1 cup ice cubes

Directions:

1. combine chopped carrots, fresh ginger, ground turmeric, coconut water, agave syrup, and ice cubes in a blender.
2. Blend until smooth and nourishing.
3. Pour into a glass and enjoy the immune-boosting benefits.

Cherry Almond Chia Frappe

Indulge in the goodness of antioxidants and omega-3s with this Cherry Almond Chia Frappe. Combining cherries, almonds, and chia seeds is a delightful and nutritious treat.

TOTAL TIME COOKING: 10 minutes

Ingredients:

- 1/2 cup cherries, pitted
- 1/4 cup almonds
- 1 tablespoon chia seeds
- 1 cup almond milk
- 1 tablespoon agave syrup or any sweetener of choice
- 1 cup ice cubes

Directions:

1. combine cherries, almonds, chia seeds, almond milk, agave syrup, and ice cubes in a blender.
2. Blend until smooth and antioxidant-rich.
3. Pour into a glass and enjoy the vibrant and nutritious frappe.

Spicy Pineapple Cilantro Frappe

Awaken your taste buds with this Spicy Pineapple Cilantro Frappe. The combination of spicy jalapeño, sweet pineapple, and fresh cilantro creates a unique and refreshing flavor profile.

TOTAL TIME COOKING: 8 minutes

Ingredients:

- 1 cup pineapple chunks
- 1/2 jalapeño, seeds removed
- Handful of fresh cilantro leaves
- Juice of 1 lime
- 1 cup coconut water
- 1 tablespoon agave syrup or honey
- 1 cup ice cubes

Directions:

1. combine pineapple chunks, jalapeño, cilantro leaves, lime juice, coconut water, agave syrup, and ice cubes in a blender.
2. Blend until smooth and spicy-sweet.
3. Pour into a glass and enjoy the refreshing flavors.

Beet Berry Protein Frappe

Fuel your day with this Beet Berry Protein Frappe. Packed with the nutritional benefits of beets, mixed berries, and plant-based protein, this frappe is a vibrant and satisfying option.

TOTAL TIME COOKING: 12 minutes (including beet preparation)

Ingredients:

- 1/2 cup cooked and peeled beets
- 1/2 cup mixed berries (strawberries, blueberries, raspberries)
- 1 scoop of plant-based protein powder
- 1 cup almond milk
- 1 tablespoon agave syrup or any sweetener of choice
- 1 cup ice cubes

Directions:

1. combine cooked beets, mixed berries, plant-based protein powder, almond milk, agave syrup, and ice cubes in a blender.
2. Blend until smooth and protein-packed.
3. Pour into a glass and enjoy the nutrient-rich goodness.

Watermelon Basil Mint Frappe

Stay cool and hydrated with this Watermelon Basil Mint Frappe. The juicy sweetness of watermelon and the herbal notes of basil and mint make it a refreshing and healthy choice.

TOTAL TIME COOKING: 8 minutes

Ingredients:

- 1 cup watermelon chunks
- Handful of fresh basil leaves
- Handful of fresh mint leaves
- Juice of 1 lime
- 1 cup coconut water
- 1 tablespoon agave syrup or honey
- 1 cup ice cubes

Directions:

1. combine watermelon chunks, basil leaves, mint leaves, lime juice, coconut water, agave syrup, and ice cubes in a blender.
2. Blend until smooth and hydrating.
3. Pour into a glass and enjoy the cooling and delicious frappe.

Green Pea Mint Detox Frappe

Detoxify your body with this Green Pea Mint Detox Frappe. This frappe is a flavorful and cleansing option, packed with green peas and fresh mint.

TOTAL TIME COOKING: 10 minutes

Ingredients:

- 1/2 cup cooked green peas
- Handful of fresh mint leaves
- Juice of 1 lemon
- 1 cup coconut water
- 1 tablespoon agave syrup or honey
- 1 cup ice cubes

Directions:

1. combine cooked green peas, mint leaves, lemon juice, coconut water, agave syrup, and ice cubes in a blender.
2. Blend until smooth and detoxifying.
3. Pour into a glass and enjoy the refreshing and revitalizing frappe.

Pumpkin Spice Chia Frappe

Embrace the fall season with this Pumpkin Spice Chia Frappe. Packed with pumpkin goodness and the warmth of spices, this frappe is a satisfying and nutrient-rich choice.

TOTAL TIME COOKING: 15 minutes (including pumpkin preparation)

Ingredients:

- 1/2 cup cooked and cooled pumpkin
- 1 teaspoon pumpkin spice blend
- 1 tablespoon chia seeds
- 1 cup almond milk
- 1 tablespoon maple syrup or agave syrup
- 1 cup ice cubes

Directions:

1. combine cooked pumpkin, pumpkin spice blend, chia seeds, almond milk, maple syrup, and ice cubes in a blender.
2. Blend until smooth and fall-inspired.
3. Pour into a glass and enjoy the seasonal flavors.

Asparagus Avocado Lime Frappe

Boost your nutrient intake with this Asparagus Avocado Lime Frappe. This frappe is a unique and nutritious beverage packed with greens and healthy fats.

TOTAL TIME COOKING: 12 minutes

Ingredients:

- 1/2 cup cooked asparagus
- 1/2 avocado
- Juice of 1 lime
- Handful of spinach leaves
- 1 cup coconut water
- 1 tablespoon agave syrup or honey
- 1 cup ice cubes

Directions:

1. combine cooked asparagus, avocado, lime juice, spinach leaves, coconut water, agave syrup, and ice cubes in a blender.
2. Blend until smooth and nutrient-dense.
3. Pour into a glass and enjoy the green goodness.

Mango Basil Quinoa Frappe

Combine the goodness of mango and quinoa with this Mango Basil Quinoa Frappe. This frappe is a satisfying and wholesome choice, packed with protein and tropical sweetness.

TOTAL TIME COOKING: 15 minutes (including quinoa preparation)

Ingredients:

- 1/2 cup cooked and cooled quinoa
- 1 cup mango chunks (fresh or frozen)
- Handful of fresh basil leaves
- 1 cup almond milk
- 1 tablespoon agave syrup or any sweetener of choice
- 1 cup ice cubes

Directions:

1. combine cooked quinoa, mango chunks, basil leaves, almond milk, agave syrup, and ice cubes in a blender.
2. Blend until smooth and protein-packed.
3. Pour into a glass and enjoy the unique combination of flavors.

Cranberry Almond Protein Frappe

Energize your day with this Cranberry Almond Protein Frappe. Packed with the tartness of cranberries and the protein punch from almonds, this frappe is a delicious and filling choice.

TOTAL TIME COOKING: 10 minutes

Ingredients:

- 1/2 cup cranberries (fresh or frozen)
- 1/4 cup almonds
- 1 scoop of plant-based protein powder
- 1 cup almond milk
- 1 tablespoon agave syrup or any sweetener of choice
- 1 cup ice cubes

Directions:

1. combine cranberries, almonds, protein powder, almond milk, agave syrup, and ice cubes in a blender.
2. Blend until smooth and energizing.
3. Pour into a glass and enjoy the vibrant and protein-rich frappe.

Printed in Great Britain
by Amazon